AF599204

AT THE CONSTRUCTION SITE
Earth Movers
by Mari Schuh
BLASTOFF! READERS
1
BELLWETHER MEDIA • MINNEAPOLIS, MN

Blastoff! Readers are carefully developed by literacy experts to build reading stamina and move students toward fluency by combining standards-based content with developmentally appropriate text.

Level 1 provides the most support through repetition of high-frequency words, light text, predictable sentence patterns, and strong visual support.

Level 2 offers early readers a bit more challenge through varied sentences, increased text load, and text-supportive special features.

Level 3 advances early-fluent readers toward fluency through increased text load, less reliance on photos, advancing concepts, longer sentences, and more complex special features.

★ **Blastoff! Universe**

Reading Level

Grade K

Grades 1–3

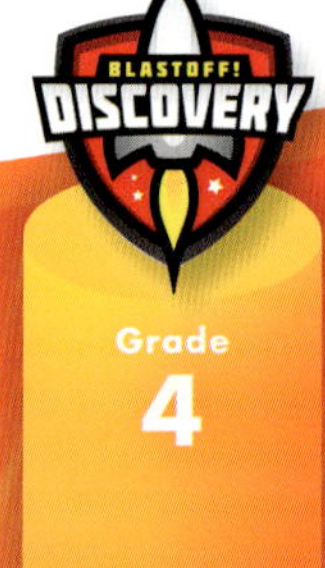

Grade 4

This edition first published in 2025 by Bellwether Media, Inc.

Library of Congress Cataloging-in-Publication Data

LC record for Earth Movers available at: https://lccn.loc.gov/2024002274

Editor: Rebecca Sabelko Designer: Josh Brink

Printed in the United States of America, North Mankato, MN.

Table of Contents

Moving Rocks

An earth mover moves rocks. It works hard at the **job site**!

job site

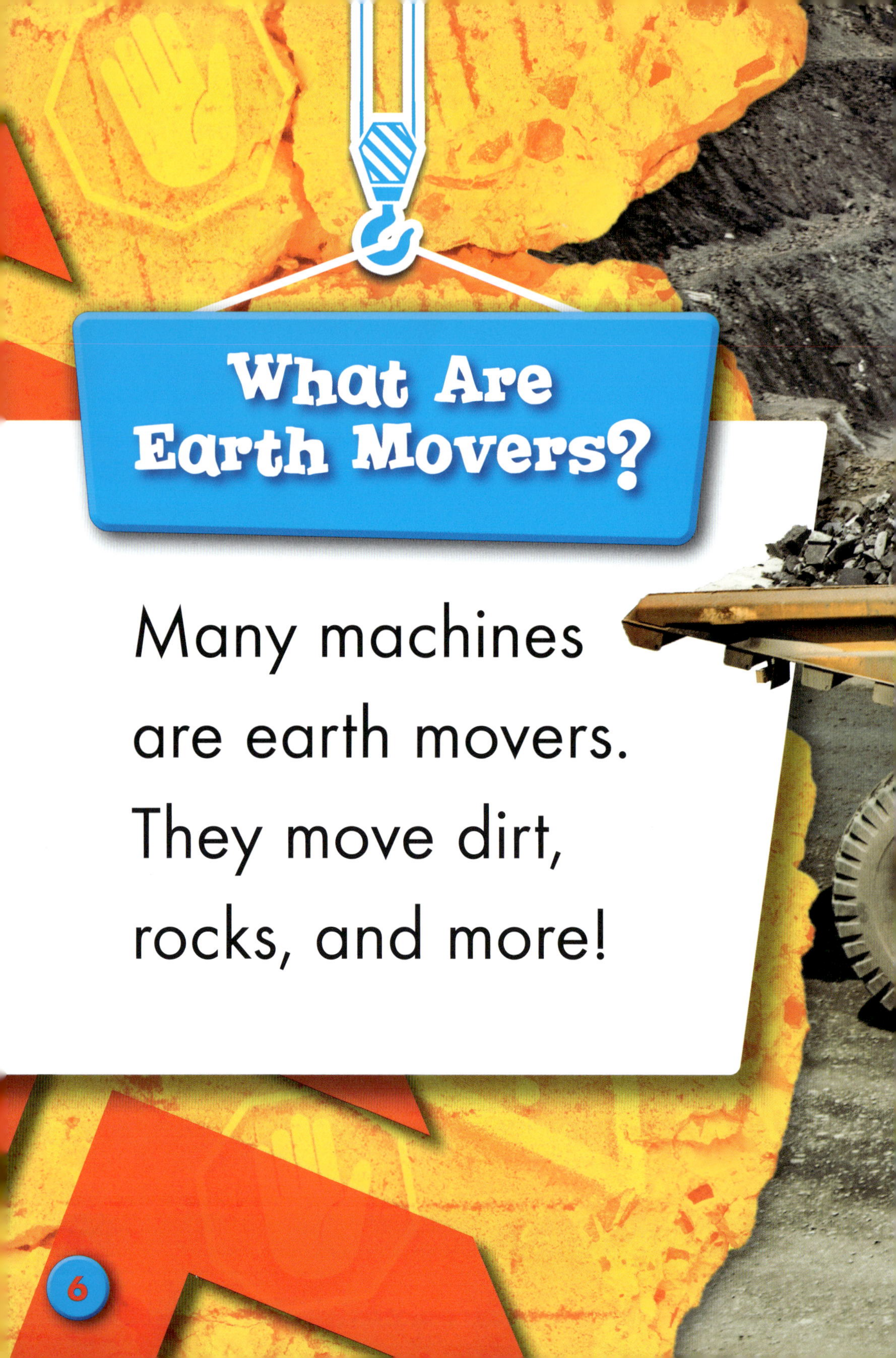

What Are Earth Movers?

Many machines are earth movers. They move dirt, rocks, and more!

13

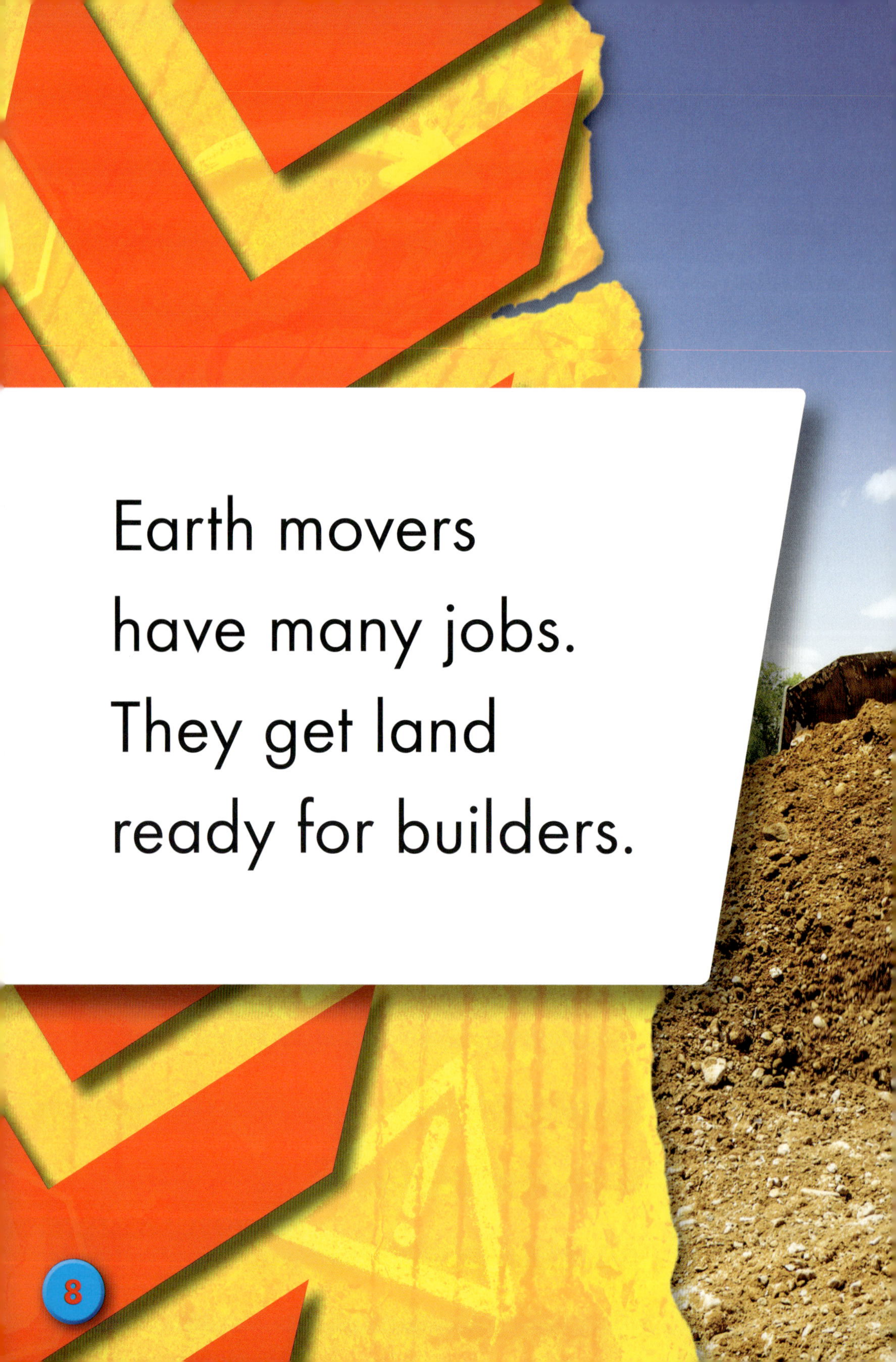

Earth movers have many jobs. They get land ready for builders.

Some earth movers dig big, deep holes. They **scoop** up rocks and dirt.

Other earth movers push dirt. Some carry dirt away.

Earth Mover Jobs
dig holes
push dirt
carry loads

Kinds of Earth Movers

Here comes a bulldozer! Its strong **blade** pushes dirt.

blade

This backhoe has a **bucket**. It digs, lifts, and moves heavy **loads**.

bucket
load

Dump trucks have a **dump box**. They carry heavy loads.

Identify an Earth Mover
blade
bucket
dump box
dump box

Look at the earth movers. They get the job done!

Glossary

blade

a strong, wide part of a bulldozer that pushes and flattens

job site

a place where bulldozers and other machines are used

bucket

the part of a backhoe that digs, lifts, and moves loads

loads

things that are carried or lifted by a machine

dump box

the part that holds a dump truck's load

scoop

to dig out

To Learn More

AT THE LIBRARY

Humphrey, Natalie. *Incredible Earthmovers.* New York, N.Y.: Gareth Stevens Publishing, 2023.

Pettiford, Rebecca. *Bulldozers.* Minneapolis, Minn.: Jump!, 2023.

Schuh, Mari. *Backhoes.* Minneapolis, Minn.: Bellwether Media, 2025.

ON THE WEB

FACTSURFER

Factsurfer.com gives you a safe, fun way to find more information.

1. Go to www.factsurfer.com.
2. Enter "earth movers" into the search box and click 🔍.
3. Select your book cover to see a list of related content.

Index

The images in this book are reproduced through the courtesy of: Kaband, front cover (hero); Yevhenii Chulovskyi, front cover (background), back cover; Oleg Rebrov, pp. 2-3, 22-24 (background); Another77, pp. 3 (loader), 19 (bucket); JaneMoon, pp. 4-5; Maksim Safaniuk, p. 5 (job site); Alexander Khorkov, pp. 6-7; Andrew Ostry, pp. 8-9; GIRODJL, pp. 10-11; MiloVad, pp. 12-13; T VECTOR ICONS, p. 13 (excavator vector, bulldozer vector); Nechayka, p. 13 (dump truck vector); horsemen, pp. 14-15; TheHighestQualityImages, pp. 16-17; Randy Hergenrether, pp. 18-19; VanderWolf Images, p. 19 (blade); Dmitry Kalinovsky, pp. 19 (bucket), 22 (bucket); ewg3D, pp. 20-21; Martin Lisner, p. 22 (blade); Nordroden, p. 22 (dump box); rsooll, p. 22 (job site); bogubogu, p. 22 (loads); Mironmax Studio, p. 22 (scoop); Valentin Valkov, p. 23 (bulldozer).